Published by HEFE 360 GLOBAL INC.

ISBN: 979-8-998-7240-0-8

This book is intended for educational and informational purposes only.

HEFE 360 GLOBAL INC. is a consulting company and does not offer licensed financial, legal, or investment services. Readers are encouraged to consult with a qualified professional before making any financial decisions.

Printed in the United States of America.

Website: www.hefe360global.com

Email: info@hefe360global.com

First Edition, 2025

Disclaimer:

This book is intended for educational and informational purposes only. HEFE 360 GLOBAL INC. is a consulting company, not a licensed financial advisor, broker, or investment firm. The strategies discussed reflect the experiences and perspectives of the author and should not be taken as legal, tax, or financial advice. Readers are encouraged to consult with qualified professionals before making any financial decisions.

Own Nothing, Control Everything: The HEFE 360 Global Wealth Strategy

📖 Table of Contents

📖 Chapter 2: The Power of Promissory Notes & How to Turn Debt into Cash Flow

✔ Why an aged corporation is a fast-track to funding

✔ How to use a Personal Guarantee (PG) to secure business credit

✔ Step-by-step business credit-building blueprint

📖 Chapter 3: Building Personal & Business Credit for Maximum Leverage

✔ How to boost personal credit (680+ FICO) to qualify for major loans

✔ How to get high-limit business credit cards and trade lines

✔ The best platforms for reporting credit and boosting scores fast

📌 **PART 2: LEVERAGING CORPORATE FINANCE & REAL ESTATE**

📖 Chapter 4: Business Credit & Scaling Business Funding

✔ Creating corporate stock certificates & valuing shares

✔ How corporations issue private bonds to raise capital

✔ How to use corporate bonds instead of bank loans

📖 Chapter 5: Investment-Grade Bonds & Private Placement for Funding

✔ What is an investment-grade bond?

✔ How bond insurance boosts security & credibility for investors

✔ The private placement process for raising capital

📖 Chapter 6: Stock Certificates & Corporate Valuation

✔ How stock certificates act as corporate money

✔ Stated Value vs. Market Value – How stock prices are determined

✔ Why transfer agents are needed for legal stock transfers

📌 PART 3: REAL ESTATE ACQUISITION & ASSET PROTECTION

📖 Chapter 7: Commercial Lending & Real Estate Funding Strategies

✔ How to use business credit to buy real estate

✔ Creating a promissory note backed by rental income

✔ How Trust 1 (Cayman) and Trust 2 (Cook Islands) hold property & promissory notes

📖 Chapter 8: Advanced Asset Protection & Offshore Banking

✔ How to set up offshore bank accounts in asset-friendly jurisdictions

✔ Why the Cook Islands provides the best legal protection

✔ Using insurance policies & IULs as a wealth shield

📌 PART 4: THE HEFE FAMILY BANKING SYSTEM

📖 Chapter 9: The HEFE Family Banking System – Infinite Generational Wealth

✔ How to use Indexed Universal Life (IULs) to create a private bank

✔ Borrowing rules: How family members can access trust funds at key ages

✔ Compound interest strategy – How wealth grows exponentially over generations

📌 PART 5: RUNNING & SCALING A BUSINESS PROPERLY

📖 Chapter 10: Corporate Governance & Robert's Rules of Order

✔ How to run a corporation using Robert's Rules of Order

✔ Writing corporate meeting minutes & resolutions

✔ What is a resolution letter, and when should you use one?

📌 PART 6: REAL-WORLD CASE STUDIES & FINAL TAKEAWAYS

📖 Chapter 11: Case Studies & Real-World Examples of Generational Wealth

✔ The Rockefeller Trust – 11+ generations of wealth

✔ The Rothschild Banking Dynasty – Controlling wealth without owning it

✔ How Walt Disney used corporate bonds to finance Disneyland

✔ Modern entrepreneurs using the HEFE Strategy to build wealth today

📌 Final Thoughts & Action Plan: Implementing the HEFE Strategy

✔ A step-by-step checklist to get started today

✔ How to set up your corporation, trusts, and business credit in 90 days

✔ Next steps: Taking action to secure generational wealth

📖 Introduction – The HEFE 360 Blueprint

🚀 Welcome to the HEFE 360 Wealth Revolution

For too long, wealth has been **a game only the rich knew how to play.**

For too long, **communities have been left out of financial education.**

For too long, people have been **trapped in a system designed to keep them struggling**—working paycheck to paycheck, never getting ahead, never learning the secrets of wealth.

💡 That ends today!

This book is more than just financial education. **It's a movement. It's a blueprint.**

This is about **breaking the cycle of financial struggle** and **creating a new legacy of wealth—for** yourself, your family, and future generations.

I wasn't born into wealth. I wasn't handed financial knowledge. **I had to learn the hard way—through research, trial, and experience.** But once I started uncovering the **secrets the wealthy use to build generational wealth,** everything changed.

And now, I'm bringing those secrets to YOU.

💰 **The Wealth Game is Rigged—Here's How You Beat It**

Most people are taught that building wealth takes a lifetime. That you need to:

❌ Work a 9-to-5 job for 40 years.

❌ Save up money for decades.

❌ Invest in slow-growing retirement accounts.

❌ Maybe—just maybe—have enough to retire.

🗿 **That's a lie. That's a system designed to keep you working, not to make you wealthy.**

The truth is, the wealthy don't play by those rules. They don't wait decades to build assets. They use corporate structures, financial leverage, and investment strategies to grow their wealth in months—not years.

Here's what **they don't tell you:**

✔ **You don't need to save $100,000 to get a $100,000 investment. You can get a $100,000 business loan TODAY with an aged corporation.**

✔ **You don't need to work for years to build business**

credit—aged corporations already come with history that banks trust.

✔ You don't need millions in the bank to access capital—you can issue corporate shares and bonds to raise funding legally.

💡 This book is about unlocking those wealth-building secrets and showing you exactly how to use them.

⏳ How Fast Can You Do This? (Months, Not Years)

Most people think it takes years to qualify for business loans, raise capital, or build wealth.

🖥 That's not true. This system can work in MONTHS.

Here's how fast things can move:

✅ Step 1: Buy an Aged Corporation (Week 1-2)

Instead of waiting 2-3 years to qualify for business loans, you can **buy an aged corporation** that already has history.

This means you **skip the waiting game and can apply for business credit & loans IMMEDIATELY.**

✅ Step 2: Secure a $100K+ Loan (Month 1-2)

Once your corporation is set up, you can apply for **$50K-$500K in business lines of credit.**

No need to work a job for years to save that money.

✅ **Step 3: Issue a $100K+ Corporate Bond (Month 2-3)**

You can use that loan to **create a promissory note & issue a corporate bond** for another $100K-$200K in capital.

This is how banks and corporations multiply money.

✅ **Step 4: Buy Real Estate or Invest in More Income-Producing Assets (Month 3-6)**

With the capital raised from bonds, you can buy a **commercial property, secure rental income, or reinvest into another business.**

This allows you to **create more promissory notes, issue more bonds, and repeat the process—multiplying your wealth.**

✅ **Step 5: Use Rental Income or Business Profits to Pay Off Debt (Month 6-12)**

Your **business or real estate assets generate cash flow**, which pays for the loans and bonds.

Instead of using y**our own paycheck, your assets are working for you.**

At this point, **you've built a financial system that funds itself.**

💡 Total Time? In 6-12 months, you can go from having ZERO capital to controlling hundreds of thousands—or even millions—of dollars in assets.

🚀 This is how the wealthy move. This is how YOU can move.

🏛 The Power of Corporate Shares & The Corporate Binder

Most people don't realize that **when you own a corporation, you have the ability to create financial instruments—just like banks and large companies do.**

◆ What is a Corporate Binder?

A corporate binder (which costs as little as $125-$150) is what holds your **corporate shares and key documents.**

Every corporation has shares—but most people don't realize that **you control how many shares your company has** and **what each share is worth.**

You can issue **1 million, 10 million, or even 100 million share**s—and assign them a dollar value. This is known as"**stated value**", not to be confused with **market value**

This is literally how money is created.

◆ Why This Matters

Instead of **working for money**, you can **create value through your corporation's shares and use them to raise capital.**

13

You can use **shares as collateral for loans.**

You can **transfer shares into a trust and use them to issue corporate bonds—just like major companies do.**

💡 **Once you understand this, you'll never think about money the same way again.**

🔥 **The Mission of HEFE 360 GLOBAL, INC.**

At **HEFE 360 GLOBAL, INC.,** we believe that **financial knowledge should not be a luxury—it should be accessible to EVERYONE.**

💡 **Our mission is simple:**

✔ **Empower the underbanked & undercredited to break free from financial limitations.**

✔ **Teach real wealth-building strategies that have been hidden from our communities.**

✔ **Create a generation of financially independent entrepreneurs & investors.**

💰 **Financial freedom is not just for the wealthy—it's for YOU, too.**

🚀 **This is YOUR time to take control.**

Welcome to **The HEFE 360 Blueprint.**

Let's build wealth, break barriers, and create legacies—**TOGETHER.**

📖 Chapter 1: The Foundation—How to Structure Your Financial Empire

🚀 Why Your Financial Structure Matters

Most people think **wealth is just about how much money you make.** That's wrong. **Wealth is about how you structure your money.**

Think about this:

❌ A person making $500,000 a year but paying **high taxes and personal debts** could be broke.

✅ Meanwhile, a person making **$100,000 through a corporation, trusts, and financial instruments** could be generating wealth tax-efficiently and legally protecting their assets.

💡 The rich don't just earn money—they structure it the right way to multiply, protect, and keep it. Just like your home or anything with building in life for that matter, is only strong as the foundation it's built on.

That's exactly what we're going to do in this chapter.

🔥 The Three Pillars of Wealth Structure

To build an unshakable financial foundation, you need **three key structures working together:**

✔ 1   A Corporation (C-Corp) → The Financial Engine

✔ 2   Trusts (Cayman & Cook Islands) → Asset Protection & Wealth Storage

✔ 3   Business Credit & Funding → The Fuel to Scale Quickly

Once you have **these three pieces in place, you can start leveraging financial instruments like bonds, promissory notes, and corporate shares.**

Let's go through them one by one.

💼 1   Why You Need a Corporation (C-Corp)

If you're serious about building wealth, **you need to stop thinking like an individual and start thinking like a corporation.** For now on you live thru the C-Corp. In essence you will, have created your very own legal strawman to do business with. We are not recreating the wheel here...we are just done what has been being done for decades upon decades now.

◆ What is a Corporation?

A corporation is a **separate legal entity** that:

Can **apply for loans and lines of credit.**

Can **own real estate and businesses.**

Can **issue shares and raise money without personal**

liability.

Can **get tax benefits that individuals can't.**

◆ Why a C-Corp Instead of an LLC or S-Corp?

☑ **C-Corps allow you to issue shares, which is the key to raising large amounts of money.**

☑ **C-Corps don't have ownership restrictions like LLCs and S-Corps do.**

☑ **C-Corps make it easier to scale your business and eventually take on investors or even go public (IPO).**

💡 **Think of your C-Corp as your wealth-building engine. It's where money flows in, gets leveraged, and gets reinvested.**

2   Trusts—The Secret to Protecting & Multiplying Wealth

Once your C-Corp is up and running, you need a **safe place to store and protect your wealth.**

That's where Trusts come in.

◆ What is a Trust?

A trust is a **legal entity that holds and protects assets on your behalf.**

It's **not owned by you**, meaning it's **protected from lawsuits, creditors, and even taxes in some cases.**

The rich use trusts to pass down wealth tax-free and shield assets from liabilities.

Trusts **can own businesses, real estate, and financial instruments (like promissory notes and corporate shares).**

💡 **Once money flows into a trust, it is legally protected and can be leveraged for even more capital.**

◆ **Why We Use Two Trusts (Cayman Islands & Cook Islands)**

To take your wealth-building strategy to the highest level, **you use two offshore trusts working together.**

✔ **Trust 1 (Cayman Islands) → Holds assets like corporate shares and promissory notes.**

✔ **Trust 2 (Cook Islands) → Uses those assets to issue corporate bonds and raise even more capital.**

◆ **Why the Cook Islands? (Legal Protection at the Highest Level)**

The Cook Islands has some of the **strongest asset protection laws in the world.**

💰 Here's the KEY advantage:

If a **U.S. court orders you to turn over trust assets,** the foreign trustee in the Cook Islands **is legally required to REFUSE.**

🔥 **This means that even if someone sues you, they cannot touch the wealth inside your Cook Islands trust.**

💡 **This is why the Rockefellers and other billionaires use similar trust structures.**

▰ 3   Business Credit & Funding—Fueling Your Financial Empire

Most people **think they need to use their own money to fund their businesses or investments.**

That's not how the wealthy move.

The wealthy **use other people's money (OPM)** to scale quickly, and they do this by:

☑️ **Using their corporation to qualify for business credit.**

☑️ **Getting business lines of credit (BLOCs) using a Personal Guarantee (PG).**

☑️ **Using funding to acquire real estate and assets that generate cash flow.**

◆ How the Personal Guarantee (PG) Works

Because your aged corporation is new to you, banks will require a **personal guarantee (PG) from an individual** to approve the first round of business credit.

🪪 **A PG means you are personally responsible for the debt if the corporation fails to pay.**

💡 **This is how you get approved for high-limit funding quickly, instead of waiting years for business credit to build.**

✅ Who Can Be the PG?

You **(the business owner)** can use your personal credit.

A **business partner or investor** with strong credit can PG instead.

✅ Credit Requirements for a PG:

680+ FICO Score (higher scores get better approvals).

Strong payment history (at least 2+ years of on-time payments).

Low credit utilization (below 30% for best results).

💡 **If you don't meet these requirements, don't worry!**

We'll cover **credit repair strategies in the Personal Credit Chapter** to help you get your score where it needs to be.

◈ **Why We Use Business Lines of Credit (BLOCs) Instead of Loans**

A Business Line of Credit (BLOC) is different from a traditional loan.

✔ Business lines of credit are NO-DOC – meaning you don't need tax returns, W-2s, or proof of income to qualify.

✔ Traditional business loans require documentation, credit checks, and tax filings – but BLOCs give instant access to cash without all the paperwork.

✔ You can use a BLOC like cash or withdraw it anytime without restrictions.

✔ We use BLOCs to immediately fund aged corporations, eliminating the waiting period for large business loans.

💡 **Key Takeaway:**

🔥 By using your personal credit as a PG, you can get a BLOC for $50K-$100K IMMEDIATELY—without tax returns, W-2s, or pay stubs.

🔥 Once the corporation is funded, you can then start applying for larger loans (if needed).

🔥 **The HEFE 360 Wealth Structure—Putting It All Together**

Let's look at the full blueprint:

◆ Step-by-Step Process for Setting Up Your Financial Empire

☑ **1   Set up your C-Corp** → The financial engine that allows you to raise money.Get an aged corporation → Skip the 2-3 year waiting period and get funding immediately.

☑ **2   Set up Trust 1 (Cayman Islands)** → Protects corporate shares and promissory notes.

☑ **3   Set up Trust 2 (Cook Islands)** → Issues corporate bonds and raises funding.

☑ **4   Secure business loans & credit** → Use OPM (other people's money) to acquire assets.

☑ **5   Buy real estate & generate passive income** → Rental income pays off debt while increasing your wealth.

☑ **6   Repeat the process** → Use financial instruments (promissory notes & bonds) to keep expanding.

💡 **Once this system is in place, your money will grow automatically, and your wealth will be protected.**

📖 Chapter 2: The Power of Promissory Notes & How to Turn Debt into Cash Flow

🚀 What is a Promissory Note?

Most people have heard of a **loan agreement**, but a **promissory note** is an even more **powerful financial tool** because:

✔ It's a **legally binding IOU** that states one party promises to pay another a set amount over time.

✔ It can be backed by an income-producing asset (like real estate or a business).

✔ It can be sold, transferred, or used as collateral to raise even more money.

💡 Think of it like this: A promissory note turns future income into immediate cash flow.

Example:

If you own a rental property that generates **$30K per month ($360K per year),** you can **create a promissory note for $1M,** backed by that rental income. **That note can then be used as collateral for a loan or turned into a corporate bond.**

🔥 This is how you legally create money from an asset you already own!

💰 How to Create a Promissory Note Backed by Rental Income

Let's break it down step by step:

Step 1: Identify the Income-Producing Asset

A **promissory note needs to be backed by something valuable.**

For this strategy, we **use real estate rental income to secure the note.**

💡 Example:

You own a **30-unit apartment building** that generates **$30K/month in rent ($360K/year).**

You create a **$1M promissory note, stating that payments will be made using rental income.**

This **$1M note is now an asset that can be used to get even more funding.**

💡 **Before we continue—don't get discouraged by large real estate numbers.** It is completely obtainable thru commercial financing which allows you to put a down payment of only 10-20% to own a commercial unit (property that has 5+ units). Example , to purchase a $2 million dollar property would require a $200k down payment (that will be obtained through corporate funding using your personal credit as a personal guarantor).

A 30-unit property valued at $2M might sound huge right now, but **with the power of corporate finance, it's completely obtainable.**

Here's why:

✔ You are not using personal savings—you're using financial instruments.

✔ Aged corporations allow you to raise $100K+ in business credit FAST.

✔ Promissory notes & corporate bonds allow you to raise $1M+ in funding.

✔ Stock certificates (corporate shares) allow you to create even MORE capital.

🔥 Once you understand and apply these strategies, acquiring multi-million-dollar assets becomes a reality.

Step 2: Use the Promissory Note as Collateral for a Loan

Now that we have a **$1M promissory note backed by rental income,** we can use it to **secure a loan.**

☑️ The promissory note is pledged as collateral to a private lender or bank.

☑️ Lenders typically offer 50-70% of the note's value as a loan.

☑️ In this case, we could get a $500K-$700K loan using the note as collateral.

💡 This gives you immediate cash without selling the property.

🔥 At this stage, you've turned rental income into a $500K-$700K loan—WITHOUT touching your own money.

Step 3: Transfer the Promissory Note to a Trust for Asset Protection

Once we've secured a loan using the **$1M promissory note**, we need to **move the note into a trust** for protection.

☑️ The **promissory note is transferred from the business to Trust 1 (Cayman Islands).**

☑️ This means **the income is now owned by the trust and protected from lawsuits & creditors.**

💡 Why This is Important:

✔ If someone sues you, they **can't touch the promissory note—it's held in an offshore trust.**

✔ The **trust can now use this note for even more financial** moves.

🔥 Now your promissory note is safe AND you've already secured a loan against it!

Step 4: Use the Promissory Note to Issue a Corporate Bond

Now that Trust 1 **holds the promissory note,** we can take things to the next level:

✅ **The trust transfers the note to Trust 2 (Cook Islands).**

✅ **Trust 2 uses the note as backing to issue a corporate bond.**

✅ **This bond is sold to investors, bringing in another $900K-$1M in funding.**

🔥 Now you've monetized the same promissory note TWICE—once as a loan, and once as a bond.

FYI

📌 Filing & Recording a Promissory Note (Legal Requirements)

To ensure a **promissory note is legally enforceable and can be used for funding,** follow these key steps:

✔ **Draft the Promissory Note Properly** – It must include:

The **loan amount** and repayment terms.

The **parties involved** (borrower & lender).

The **asset securing the note (if applicable)**—e.g., rental property.

✔ **Notarization & Witnesses** – A **notary public** should witness the signing to verify authenticity.

✔ **File with the County Recorder's Office** – If the note is secured by real estate, **record it in the county where the property is located.**

✔ **UCC-1 Filing with the Secretary of State** – If the note is used as **collateral for a loan,** file a **UCC-1 Financing Statement** with the **Secretary of State** to secure the lender's interest in the note.

💡 Once properly filed, the promissory note becomes a legally binding financial instrument, making it eligible for collateralization, asset transfers, and bond issuance.

Chapter 3: 🚀 The Power of Personal Credit – Building & Leveraging It for Business Success

Why Personal Credit is the Key to Business Funding

Your personal credit score is a 🔑 factor in securing business funding. Here's why:

Personal Guarantees (PGs): Lenders often require a personal guarantee from business owners, especially for new businesses. This means your personal credit backs the business loan.

Access to Capital: A strong personal credit profile can unlock substantial funding amounts, often ranging from $50,000 to $100,000 or more, without the need for income verification.

Accelerated Business Credit: Solid personal credit can expedite the process of establishing business credit, bypassing the typical 2-3 year waiting period.

Understanding Personal Credit – The 5 Key Factors That Matter

Your personal credit score is determined by five main factors:

1. Payment History (35%): Timely payments are crucial. Even a single late payment can negatively impact your score.

2. Credit Utilization (30%): This refers to the ratio of your credit card balances to credit limits. Keeping this ratio below 30% is advisable.

3. Length of Credit History (15%): Long-standing accounts contribute positively to your score. It's beneficial to maintain older accounts.

4. New Credit Inquiries (10%): Frequent applications for new credit can temporarily lower your score.

5. Credit Mix (10%): A diverse range of credit accounts, such as credit cards, mortgages, and installment loans, can enhance your score.

How to Fix & Improve Your Credit Score

If your credit score is below 680, consider the following strategies to enhance it:

1. Remove Negative Items from Your Credit Report:

Obtain Your Credit Reports: Access your reports from Equifax, Experian, and TransUnion through AnnualCreditReport.com.

Dispute Inaccuracies: Challenge any incorrect or outdated information. The Fair Credit Reporting Act (FCRA) mandates the removal of unverifiable or inaccurate items.

Validate Debts: Request debt validation from collection agencies. If they can't verify the debt, they are obligated to remove it.

2. Add Positive Accounts (Tradelines) to Your Credit Report:

Authorized User (AU) Accounts: Being added as an authorized user on a creditworthy individual's account can boost your score.

Secured Credit Cards: These cards require a deposit and can help rebuild credit when used responsibly.

Credit Builder Loans: Offered by some financial institutions, these loans are designed to help individuals build credit.

Rent Reporting Services: Services like Boom report your on -time rent payments to major credit bureaus, aiding in credit building.

Tradeline Platforms: Platforms like Kikoff offer credit-building accounts that can help improve your credit score.

3. Lower Your Credit Utilization:

Pay Down Balances: Reducing credit card balances can improve your utilization ratio, positively impacting your score.

Increase Credit Limits: Requesting higher credit limits can also lower your utilization percentage, provided spending doesn't increase correspondingly.

Using Personal Credit to Secure Business Funding

With a personal credit score of 680 or higher, you can leverage it to obtain business funding:

Business Lines of Credit (BLOC): Lenders may offer substantial credit lines based on your personal creditworthiness.

Personal Guarantees (PG): Your personal credit serves as collateral, facilitating access to business capital.

Strategic Investment: Utilize the acquired funds to grow your business or invest in assets, propelling business success.

Summary

A robust personal credit profile is foundational for accessing business funding. By understanding credit factors and implementing improvement strategies, you can enhance your creditworthiness and unlock financial opportunities for your business.

📖 Chapter 4: Business Credit & Scaling Business Funding

🚀 Why Business Credit is a Game-Changer

Most people never learn about business credit because schools and traditional financial systems don't teach it.

💡 The truth is, businesses can build credit SEPARATE from personal credit—allowing you to access massive funding without using your SSN or personal guarantees forever.

✔ Business credit lets you borrow money in your company's name—without personal risk.

✔ You can access six-figure credit limits even if you don't have great personal credit.

✔ Major corporations use business credit to scale, and YOU can do the same.

🔥 If you learn how to properly establish and grow business credit, you'll never have to rely on your personal credit again.

📊 Business Credit vs. Personal Credit – What's the Difference?

Most people assume business credit works the same way as personal credit. That's FALSE.

◆ Personal Credit (FICO Score) → Based on your SSN, credit history, and personal spending habits.

◆ Business Credit (PAYDEX & Business Credit Scores) → Based on your EIN (Employer Identification Number) and your company's financial activity.

Key Differences:

✅ Business credit limits are MUCH higher than personal credit. (Banks may give a $50K business credit card vs. a $10K personal credit card.)

✅ Business credit can be built FASTER than personal credit. (A new business can establish credit in months, not years.)

✅ Business credit protects personal assets. (If structured correctly, defaults won't impact your personal credit.)

🔥 This is how wealthy business owners obtain millions in

funding—WITHOUT personal risk.

🏦 Step 1: Setting Up Your Business for Credit Success

Before you can apply for business credit, you must properly structure your business.

✅ Register Your Business as an C-Corp → Sole proprietors don't qualify for real business credit.

✅ Obtain an EIN from the IRS → This is like a Social Security Number, but for your business.

✅ Get a DUNS Number from Dun & Bradstreet → This is required to build business credit.

✅ Open a Business Bank Account → Never mix personal and business finances.

✅ Set Up a Professional Business Presence → Business phone number, email, and website (no Gmail or Yahoo emails).

How SIC Codes Affect Business Lending

1. Risk Assessment – Banks use SIC codes to classify industries by risk level. High-risk industries (e.g., real estate investing, adult entertainment, gambling, or certain financial services) may face more loan denials or higher

interest rates.

2. Underwriting & Compliance – Some SIC codes automatically disqualify businesses from loans or merchant accounts.

3. Creditworthiness – If a business is misclassified under a high-risk SIC code, it can hurt funding opportunities.

High-Risk SIC Codes (Difficult to Get Loans)

Real Estate Investing (6531) – Often seen as speculative and high-risk.

Finance & Lending (6111, 6141, 6153) – Banks may not lend to financial services businesses.

Gambling (7999) – Includes online betting and casinos.

CBD & Cannabis (5122, 2833, 2836, 5122, 7389) – Restricted by federal banking laws.

Low-Risk SIC Codes (Easier to Get Loans)

Consulting (8742, 8748) – Business and management consulting.

IT Services (7371, 7379) – Software development, cybersecurity, and IT consulting.

Healthcare (8011, 8099) – Medical practices and health services.

Construction (1521, 1711) – General contractors and specialty trades.

How to Check or Change Your SIC Code

1. Look Up Your Business SIC Code – Check it on the Dun & Bradstreet (D&B) website or your business credit report (Experian, Equifax, or D&B).

2. Change It If Necessary – If your SIC code is high-risk,

you can update it with the IRS, Dun & Bradstreet, and your bank to reflect a lower-risk industry.

💡 Banks and lenders look at these factors when deciding whether to approve your business for credit.

💳 Step 2: Getting Business Credit – The First $50K+

Once your business is properly set up, you can start applying for business credit.

1   Start with Vendor Credit (Net 30 Accounts)

Net 30 vendors extend credit to new businesses even with NO history. They report payments to business credit bureaus like Dun & Bradstreet (D&B).

💡 Examples of Net 30 Vendors:

✔ Uline – Office & warehouse supplies (www.uline.com)

✔ Grainger – Industrial supplies (www.grainger.com) hi

✔ Quill – Office supplies (www.quill.com)

☑ Order products on credit and pay within 30 days. This

builds your business credit profile FAST.

2   Apply for Business Credit Cards

Once you have a few Net 30 accounts reporting, apply for business credit cards.

💡 Top Business Credit Cards (No PG Required Over Time):

✔ Divvy Business Card (www.getdivvy.com)

✔ Ramp Business Card (www.ramp.com)

✔ Capital One Spark Business (www.capitalone.com)

🔥 These cards start reporting to business credit bureaus, helping you build a strong profile.

3   Apply for Business Lines of Credit (BLOCs)

Once your business has at least 3-6 months of strong payment history, you can apply for a business line of credit (BLOC).

💡 Top Banks for Business Lines of Credit:

✔ Bank of America – Offers up to $100K BLOCs

✔ Chase Bank – Great for businesses with consistent revenue

✔ BlueVine – Online lender, easier approval for newer businesses

✅ A BLOC is revolving credit, meaning you can borrow and repay multiple times—just like a credit card.

🚀 Step 3: Scaling Business Credit to Fund Big Investments

Once you have a solid business credit profile, you can start using it for major purchases.

Using Business Credit for Real Estate

🔥 Example: You get a $250K BLOC and use it for a down payment on an investment property.

Property generates $5K/month rental income.

Rent pays off the BLOC balance while you build equity.

Once paid down, BLOC can be reused for the next deal.

💡 This is how real estate investors acquire multiple properties without using their own cash.

Using Business Credit for Vehicles

🔥 Example: You use a business auto loan to purchase a luxury car or fleet vehicles.

Vehicle is registered under the business, protecting your personal credit.

Business tax write-offs reduce the cost.

After a few payments, the business qualifies for even higher credit limits.

💡 This is how entrepreneurs drive exotic cars without impacting personal credit.

Using Business Credit for Investments

🔥 Example: You use a business credit card or BLOC to fund inventory, marketing, or new business ventures.

Since it's business credit, personal assets aren't at risk.

As revenue grows, profits pay off the credit balance.

Credit limits increase over time, allowing for bigger investments.

💡 This is how businesses scale from small startups to multi-million-dollar enterprises.

🔥 Summary – Why Business Credit is the Ultimate Wealth Tool

💰 Business credit gives you access to large amounts of funding WITHOUT personal liability.

📈 If structured correctly, you can scale your credit limits to six figures in a matter of months.

🗓️ This is how wealthy entrepreneurs fund real estate, vehicles, and businesses without using personal money.

🔥 Once you understand business credit, you can create wealth ON DEMAND.

📖 Chapter 5: Corporate Bonds & Raising Capital Like a Bank

🚀 What is a Corporate Bond?

A corporate bond is a financial instrument that allows a business to raise money from investors in exchange for interest payments.

💡 Think of it like this: Instead of taking a bank loan, a company can issue bonds to investors who lend the company money. In return, the company pays investors a fixed interest rate (called a coupon) over a set period of time.

✔ Bonds allow businesses to raise millions WITHOUT giving up ownership (equity).

✔ Bonds can be backed by real estate, promissory notes, or corporate shares.

✔ Investors like bonds because they provide fixed returns and are secured by business assets.

🔥 Banks and large corporations raise BILLIONS through

bond issuances—this is how you can do the same.

💰 How Do Corporate Bonds Work? (Step-by-Step Example)

1   A company needs to raise $1M for an expansion.

2   Instead of getting a bank loan, they issue a $1M corporate bond.

3   Investors buy the bond, essentially lending the company money.

4   The company agrees to pay investors a fixed interest rate (coupon), such as 8% per year.

5   After a set term (e.g., 5-10 years), the company repays the bond's full value.

🔥 This is how corporations raise capital without losing control of their business.

📊 Step 1: Understanding Investment-Grade Ratings

Not all bonds are created equal. Investors will look at the creditworthiness of your bond before buying.

Credit rating agencies like Moody's, Standard & Poor's (S&P), and Fitch assign ratings to bonds based on risk.

Investment-Grade Bonds (Low Risk, High Credibility)

Moody's: Aaa, Aa, A, Baa

S&P/Fitch: AAA, AA, A, BBB

Junk Bonds (Higher Risk, Higher Interest Rates)

Moody's: Ba, B, Caa, Ca, C

S&P/Fitch: BB, B, CCC, CC, C, D

💡 Investment-grade bonds (Baa3/BBB- or higher) attract more investors and better interest rates. Lower-rated bonds must offer higher interest (yield) to attract investors.

🔥 If your company can secure an investment-grade rating, your bond becomes more valuable!

🏛 Step 2: Structuring Your Corporate Bond

Before issuing a bond, you need to structure it correctly to attract investors.

☑ Decide the Bond Amount – How much capital do you want to raise? ($500K? $1M? $5M?)

☑ Set the Bond Term – How long will the bond last? (5 years? 10 years?)

☑ Determine the Coupon Rate – What interest rate will you offer investors? (6%? 8%? 10%?)

☑ Choose What Secures the Bond – Will it be backed by real estate, promissory notes, or corporate shares?

💡 Example:

You create a $1M corporate bond with a 5-year term and an 8% coupon rate, backed by rental income from a 30-unit property.

☑ Investors know they'll receive 8% annually on their investment.

☑ At the end of 5 years, they'll get back their full principal.

🔥 This is a win-win for both the business and the investors.

📠 Step 3: Getting Investment-Grade Insurance on Your Bond

One way to make your bond more attractive to investors is to get it insured by a highly rated insurance company.

✔ If the bond is insured, investors know they'll still get paid—even if something goes wrong.

✔ This increases the bond's credibility and makes it easier to sell.

✔ Bonds with investment-grade insurance receive higher ratings, making them more valuable.

💡 Example:

A company creates a $5M bond and gets it insured by a firm like Assured Guaranty (one of the top bond insurers). Investors feel safer knowing their money is protected.

🔥 This is how major corporations and municipalities raise capital with minimal risk.

💰 Step 4: Finding Companies That Help Issue Bonds

Issuing a corporate bond is a complex process. Several specialized firms help businesses structure and launch bond offerings.

💡 Top Companies That Assist in Bond Issuance:

✔ PNC Capital Markets – Helps businesses with debt private placements & bond offerings. (pnc.com)

✔ Apex Group – Provides corporate bond structuring and compliance across various industries. (apexgroup.com)

✔ Rödl & Partner – Offers consulting for SMEs issuing bonds, including coordination with rating agencies. (roedl.com)

🔥 These firms can guide your company through the bond issuance process and help attract investors.

🔄 Step 5: How Private Placement Services Work

A private placement is when a company sells securities (like bonds) directly to investors instead of through a public stock exchange.

Why Use a Private Placement Instead of an IPO?

✔ Faster & Cheaper – No SEC registration, fewer regulations.

✔ More Control – The business decides who can invest.

✔ Great for Corporate Bonds – Investors prefer private placements for bond investments.

💡 PNC Capital Markets specializes in private placements, helping businesses raise capital from private investors. (pnc.com)

🔥 If structured correctly, businesses can raise millions in just months.

🚀 Step 6: Using the Bond as Collateral for Even More Funding

Once a corporate bond is issued, it can also be used as collateral for loans.

✔ If a business issues a $1M bond, they can often get a $500K-$700K loan against it.

✔ This allows the company to get even more funding while keeping the bond income.

✔ Banks prefer lending against bonds because they are legally binding debt instruments.

💡 Example:

A company issues a $2M bond and then uses it as collateral to secure a $1M loan for expansion.

🔥 This is how financial institutions keep leveraging capital to grow rapidly.

🔥 Summary – How You Can Raise Millions with Bonds

✔ Instead of relying on banks, businesses issue corporate bonds to raise capital.

✔ Bonds are secured by assets like rental income, corporate shares, or promissory notes.

✔ Getting bond insurance makes them safer and more attractive to investors.

✔ Bonds can be used as collateral to secure even more funding.

✔ Private placements allow businesses to raise millions without public stock offerings.

🔥 Now you know how corporations raise money like banks—and how you can do the same.

📖 Chapter 6: Stock Certificates & Leveraging Corporate Shares for Capital 🚀

💼 Customizing Your Corporation: Selecting Share Quantity

When establishing a corporation, you have the flexibility to determine the number of shares to authorize. This decision impacts ownership distribution and potential fundraising capabilities.

Considerations:

✔ Ownership Structure: Allocating shares influences control and decision-making within the company.

✔ Capital Raising: More authorized shares can facilitate future fundraising efforts.

By carefully selecting the number of shares, business owners can strategically plan for ownership retention, future investors, and business expansion.

🗂 The Importance of a Corporate Binder

A corporate binder is an essential organizational tool that maintains all critical corporate documents in one place. This includes articles of incorporation, bylaws, meeting minutes, and stock certificates.

Benefits:

✔ Organization: Keeps all vital documents systematically arranged.

✔ Compliance: Ensures adherence to legal requirements by maintaining accurate records.

✔ Accessibility: Facilitates easy access to documents for reference or audits.

A corporate binder is particularly important when dealing with investors, securing loans, or undergoing audits, as it demonstrates proper corporate governance.

📈 Understanding Share Valuation: Stated Value vs. Market Value

Shares possess different valuations that serve distinct purposes:

1   Stated Value

📌 Definition: An arbitrary value assigned by the company's board for internal accounting purposes.

📌 Significance: Used for balance sheet reporting and has little to do with real market value.

📌 Example: A company may issue 1,000,000 shares at a stated value of $0.01 per share for accounting purposes.

2   Market Value

📌 Definition: The price investors are willing to pay for shares based on the company's financial health, assets, and market conditions.

📌 Significance: Determined by supply and demand, company earnings, and asset acquisitions.

📌 Example: If a company acquires a valuable property or increases profitability, its shares may increase in market value.

Key Differences:

✔ Purpose: Stated value is used for accounting; market value reflects real-time investor sentiment.

✔ Magnitude: Stated value is typically low; market value can fluctuate significantly based on business performance.

📌 Reference: Investopedia – Stated Value

📝 Example: How Share Valuation Can Increase

The value of a company's shares can significantly increase following strategic business decisions, such as acquiring valuable assets. Consider the following scenario:

1. Initial Share Issuance:

Shares Issued: 1,000,000

Initial Share Price: $1

Initial Company Valuation: $1,000,000

2. Asset Acquisition:

The company purchases a commercial property valued at $4,000,000.

This acquisition increases the company's overall asset base and potential revenue generation.

3. Post-Acquisition Valuation:

New Company Valuation: $5,000,000 (original $1,000,000 + $4,000,000 property)

Revised Share Price: $5 per share ($5,000,000 ÷ 1,000,000 shares)

This example illustrates how strategic acquisitions can enhance a company's valuation and, consequently, increase the market value of its shares.

📌 Reference: FE Training – Asset Step-Ups in M&A

🔑 Controlling Interest: Majority Shareholders & Ownership

Holding a majority of a company's shares gives significant control over corporate decisions.

Ownership Thresholds:

✔ 80% Ownership: Ensures absolute control, allowing unilateral decision-making.

✔ 51% Ownership: Provides majority control, enabling influence over corporate policies and direction.

Implications:

✔ Decision Authority: Majority shareholders can appoint board members and dictate strategic initiatives.

✔ Minority Rights: Minority shareholders have limited influence but are protected by certain legal rights.

Understanding these ownership thresholds is crucial when structuring corporate governance.

Voting vs. Non-Voting Shares

Companies may issue different classes of shares with varying voting rights:

✔ Voting Shares: Grant shareholders the right to vote on corporate matters, such as electing directors or approving major transactions.

✔ Non-Voting Shares: Do not provide voting rights but may offer other benefits, like higher dividends or priority payouts in case of liquidation.

Considerations:

✔ Control: Voting shares are essential for those seeking influence over corporate governance.

✔ Investment Strategy: Non-voting shares might appeal to investors focused on financial returns rather than decision-making power.

This structure allows companies to raise capital without diluting control.

🧮 The Role of Trusts & Holding Companies in Managing Shares

Shares can be held by entities like trusts and holding companies, offering strategic advantages:

✔ Trusts:

Legal arrangements where trustees manage assets, including shares, for beneficiaries.

Offers tax benefits and asset protection.

✔ Holding Companies:

Parent corporations that own voting stock in other companies to control management and policies.

Streamlines operations and centralizes control.

Benefits:

✔ Asset Protection: Separates personal assets from business liabilities.

✔ Tax Efficiency: Potentially reduces tax liabilities through strategic planning.

✔ Control: Facilitates consolidated management of multiple business interests.

This structure is commonly used by wealthy families and corporations to preserve generational wealth.

🔄 Using a Transfer Agent for Stock Management

A transfer agent is a third-party entity appointed by a company to manage and maintain records of its stock ownership.

Key Responsibilities:

✔ Record Maintenance: Keeping an up-to-date register of shareholders.

✔ Certificate Management: Issuing, transferring, and canceling stock certificates as ownership changes occur.

✔ Dividend Distribution: Handling the payment of dividends to shareholders.

✔ Communication: Facilitating the dissemination of essential information, such as annual reports and voting materials.

Notable Transfer Agents:

✔ Equiniti (EQ): Provides comprehensive transfer agent services. (Equiniti)

✔ Colonial Stock Transfer: Offers stock transfer services, including issuance, transfer processing, and record maintenance. (Colonial Stock Transfer)

📌 Reference: Investopedia – Transfer Agents

💡 Enhancing Net Worth Through Share Transfers

Transferring shares to personal accounts or trusts can positively impact an individual's net worth:

✔ Direct Ownership: Holding shares personally reflects directly in one's net worth statement.

✔ Trust Ownership: Transferring shares to a trust can

provide estate planning benefits and potentially reduce estate taxes.

Steps to Transfer Shares:

1   Consult Professionals: Engage legal and financial advisors.

2   Valuation: Assess the current market value of shares.

3   Documentation: Execute legal documents for transfer.

4   Recording: Update corporate records.

Considerations:

✔ Tax Implications: Transfers may trigger tax events.

✔ Control: Ensure alignment with desired asset management goals.

This strategy is commonly used by high-net-worth individuals to protect and grow their wealth.

🔥 Chapter 7: Commercial Lending & The Power of Business Credit for Real Estate 🚀

📇 How to Obtain Commercial Lending Through Business Credit

One of the most powerful ways to acquire real estate without using personal savings is by leveraging commercial lending through business credit. Instead of relying on personal funds, a properly structured C-Corp can secure business lines of credit (BLOCs), loans, and other funding sources to purchase income-generating properties.

📌 How This Works in Simple Steps:

✔ Step 1: Obtain a business line of credit (BLOC) under the C-Corp with a Personal Guarantee (PG).

✔ Step 2: Use the funds from the BLOC as a down payment on a commercial property.

✔ Step 3: Once the property is acquired, transfer ownership into Trust 1 (Cayman Islands).

✔ Step 4: Trust 1 creates a promissory note based on the property's income.

✔ Step 5: The promissory note is transferred to Trust 2 (Cook Islands), which holds it as a financial asset.

✔ Step 6: The promissory note in Trust 2 is leveraged to create a corporate bond or raise more capital.

🔥 This cycle allows an investor to continue acquiring properties and scaling their wealth without ever using personal money.

💰 Step 1: Getting a Business Line of Credit (BLOC) Under a C-Corp

The first step in this strategy is obtaining a business line of credit (BLOC). A BLOC is a revolving source of funding that businesses can draw from and repay over time—similar to a credit card but with higher limits and lower interest rates.

How to Qualify for a BLOC Using a C-Corp

📌 Strong Business Credit: The C-Corp must be aged (2-3 years old) and have a clean credit profile with reporting agencies like Dun & Bradstreet (D&B). But preferably with no EIN number attached. This ensures there is no bad credit history.

📌 Personal Guarantee (PG): Most banks require a PG from the owner (usually a 680+ FICO score).

📌 Business Financials: While not always required, some banks may ask for business revenue statements or tax returns.

💡 Example: A newly formed C-Corp with an 80+ PAYDEX score (D&B business credit rating) and a PG from an owner with a 700 FICO score can qualify for a $250,000 BLOC.

📌 Top Banks for Business Lines of Credit:

✔ Bank of America – High-limit BLOCs for businesses with strong credit.

✔ Chase Bank – Offers flexible repayment terms and revolving credit lines.

✔ PNC Bank – Specializes in commercial real estate business credit.

🚀 Once the BLOC is secured, it's time to put that funding to work!

📅 Step 2: Using Business Credit to Acquire a Commercial Property

Now that the C-Corp has secured a business line of credit (BLOC), the next step is acquiring a commercial property.

✔ The BLOC is used as the down payment (typically 10-20%) on a commercial property.

✔ A commercial loan covers the remaining balance (80-90%) of the purchase price.

✔ The property generates rental income to cover loan payments and additional investments.

💡 Example:

Purchase Price: $2,500,000

Business Line of Credit Used for Down Payment: $250,000 (10%)

Commercial Loan Financed: $2,250,000 (90%)

Monthly Rental Income: $30,000

Loan Payment & Expenses: $18,000

Net Cash Flow: $12,000/month

🔥 This property now becomes an income-generating asset that can be leveraged for even more funding.

🏛 Step 3: Creating a Promissory Note from the Rental Income

Once the property is acquired, it is transferred into Trust 1 (Cayman Islands).

✔ Trust 1 becomes the legal owner of the property.

✔ Trust 1 creates a promissory note based on the rental income generated by the property.

✔ The promissory note is a legally binding document promising to pay an investor over time.

💡 Example:

Monthly Rental Income: $30,000

Promissory Note Value: $3,600,000 (30-year note, $10K/month at 10% interest)

The note is backed by the cash flow from the property.

🔥 This promissory note now becomes a financial asset that can be leveraged further.

🔄 Step 4: Transferring the Promissory Note to Trust 2 (Cook Islands)

✔ Trust 1 signs the promissory note over to Trust 2 (Cook Islands).

✔ Trust 2 now holds the promissory note as a financial instrument.

✔ This allows Trust 2 to use the note as collateral for more funding.

💡 Why Do This?

Asset Protection: The Cook Islands has some of the strongest trust protection laws.

Leverage: The promissory note can be used to secure more funding or issue corporate bonds.

🚀 Now that the promissory note is in Trust 2, it's time to use it to raise even more capital.

🏢 Step 5: Leveraging the Promissory Note to Create a Corporate Bond

With the promissory note securely held by Trust 2, the next step is leveraging it to issue corporate bonds.

✔ The $3,600,000 promissory note is used as collateral.

✔ Trust 2 issues a corporate bond valued at 80% of the note's worth.

✔ Investors purchase the corporate bond, providing even more capital.

💡 Example:

$3,600,000 promissory note used as collateral.

Trust 2 issues a corporate bond for $2,880,000 (80% of note value).

Investors buy the bond, providing $2,880,000 in liquid capital.

💧 This is how financial institutions create wealth—by continuously leveraging assets for more funding.

🚀 Final Breakdown: How This Model Creates Unlimited Funding

✔ Business credit funds the down payment on a commercial property.

✔ The property generates rental income and is transferred to Trust 1.

✔ Trust 1 creates a promissory note backed by the rental income.

✔ The promissory note is transferred to Trust 2.

✔ Trust 2 uses the promissory note to issue a corporate bond.

✔ Investors purchase the bond, generating millions in new funding.

💡 Each time this process is repeated, funding is continuously created without personal money ever being used!

🔥 This is how major corporations and real estate investors scale their wealth on autopilot.

📖 Summary: Using Commercial Lending & Business Credit to Scale

✔ Commercial lending allows businesses to acquire real estate using business credit instead of personal funds.

✔ A properly structured trust system maximizes financial protection and funding opportunities.

✔ Promissory notes backed by rental income create financial instruments that can be leveraged.

✔ Trusts and corporate bonds allow for continuous reinvestment and funding expansion.

🔥 By mastering this strategy, anyone can acquire multi-million dollar properties using financial leverage!

🔥 Chapter 8: Advanced Asset Protection Strategies – "ONCE" (Own Nothing, Control Everything) & The HEFE Strategy 🚀

📖 What You'll Learn in Chapter 8:

✔ How to set up an offshore asset protection structure that shields wealth legally.

✔ How to use LLCs, Trusts, and International Banking to "Own Nothing, Control Everything" (ONCE).

✔ Why Indexed Universal Life (IUL) policies are one of the best-kept secrets of the wealthy.

✔ How to use IULs as tax-free investment vehicles and family banking systems.

✔ How to set up offshore business accounts & private banking strategies.

✔ Why HEFE 360 GLOBAL INC uses this strategy as its foundation for wealth-building.

🏛 The Foundation of Advanced Asset Protection – "ONCE" (Own Nothing, Control Everything)

💡 What does "ONCE" mean?

✔ The wealthiest people and corporations do not "own" their assets personally. Instead, their assets are held in trusts, LLCs, and corporations, allowing them to control the assets while legally separating them from personal liability.

✔ This structure prevents lawsuits, protects assets from creditors, and reduces taxation while keeping full control of the wealth.

🔥 How the ONCE Strategy Works:

✔ Step 1: A person forms a C-Corp or LLC to conduct business.

✔ Step 2: The corporation owns the assets, such as real estate, business interests, and investments.

✔ Step 3: A trust (such as an offshore asset protection trust) owns the corporation, creating legal separation.

✔ Step 4: The person remains the trustee or beneficiary, meaning they still control everything.

✔ Step 5: Assets are held in offshore accounts or tax-advantaged life insurance policies (IULs).

🔥 The result? The individual owns nothing on paper, but controls everything in reality.

🌑 Setting Up Offshore Banking for Maximum Protection

Why use offshore banks?

✔ Asset Protection: Many countries offer stronger banking privacy laws than the U.S.

✔ Lawsuit Protection: Offshore assets are harder to seize in legal disputes.

✔ Global Investment Access: Offshore banks offer investment opportunities that may not be available domestically.

✔ Currency Diversification: Protect wealth from currency fluctuations.

📌 Best Countries for Offshore Banking & Asset Protection

✔ Cayman Islands – Strong banking secrecy, tax-neutral environment, no exchange controls.

✔ Cook Islands – One of the best jurisdictions for offshore trusts, nearly bulletproof asset protection.

✔ Switzerland – A historically strong banking system with secure, stable accounts.

✔ Singapore – A rising financial hub with excellent banking privacy and global investment access.

✔ Belize – Strong offshore banking laws with high interest rates on savings.

🔥 How to Open an Offshore Bank Account:

✔ Step 1: Form an offshore LLC or Trust.

✔ Step 2: Select a banking jurisdiction based on asset protection goals.

✔ Step 3: Provide business documents, trust agreements, and proof of funds.

✔ Step 4: Fund the account with an initial deposit.

📌 Important Note: U.S. citizens must report offshore accounts exceeding $10,000 under FBAR (Foreign Bank Account Report) laws and FATCA (Foreign Account Tax Compliance Act).

📌 Recommended Offshore Banks for Business & Wealth Protection:

✔ Cayman National Bank (Cayman Islands) – Trusted private banking for corporations and high-net-worth individuals.

✔ Bank of Singapore (Singapore) – Great for investment banking and international businesses.

✔ Citi Private Bank (Switzerland) – High-level banking for asset protection.

🏦 How Life Insurance (IULs) Are Used for Wealth Protection & Tax-Free Growth

🔥 The HEFE Strategy: Using IULs as the Ultimate Wealth Vehicle

What is an Indexed Universal Life (IUL) policy?

✔ A life insurance policy that builds cash value and earns

interest based on stock market performance.

✔ Unlike traditional investments, IULs grow tax-free and allow tax-free withdrawals.

✔ Cash value can be used as collateral for loans (just like business credit or real estate).

✔ Wealthy individuals use IULs as "private banking" systems.

📌 Why IULs Are the Secret of the Rich

✔ Tax-Free Growth – Earnings in the policy are NOT taxed.

✔ Tax-Free Loans – Borrow against the cash value without triggering taxes.

✔ No Stock Market Losses – If the market crashes, the policy guarantees a 0% floor (no losses).

✔ Creditor & Lawsuit Protection – In most states, IUL cash values are protected from lawsuits and creditors.

📌 Example:

A person funds an IUL with $100,000 over time. The cash value grows tax-free and reaches $500,000.

✔ The policyholder borrows $250,000 from the policy tax-free and invests in real estate.

✔ The loan never has to be repaid—it's deducted from the death benefit.

✔ No credit check, no approval needed—the person borrows from their own bank.

🔥 This is how the wealthy use IULs as a tax-free financial system for themselves.

📌 Best IUL Providers:

✔ Penn Mutual – One of the most competitive IULs in the industry.

✔ MassMutual – Great for building long-term wealth and estate planning.

✔ Nationwide – Flexible policies with strong growth potential.

💼 How Trusts & Holding Companies Protect Business Assets

🔥 How HEFE 360 GLOBAL INC Uses This Strategy

✔ Trust 1 (Cayman Islands) holds valuable assets such as real estate and intellectual property.

✔ Trust 2 (Cook Islands) holds financial instruments, such as promissory notes and bonds.

✔ The C-Corp operates the business but owns no high-risk assets directly.

✔ Insurance (IULs) store excess capital safely and allow tax-free access.

Why This Works:

✔ If a lawsuit is filed against the business, the assets are untouchable because they are held by trusts.

✔ The owner legally controls the assets through trust agreements but does not "own" them personally.

✔ Profits from real estate, investments, and business activities are funneled into tax-advantaged structures.

🚀 Summary: The HEFE Strategy for Advanced Asset Protection

✔ "ONCE" – Own Nothing, Control Everything: The key to long-term wealth protection.

✔ Offshore Banking & Asset Protection: Where to bank & how to set up secure accounts.

✔ IUL Policies for Wealth Growth & Tax-Free Income: How to become your own bank.

✔ Trusts & Corporate Structures: How to keep assets out of lawsuits and creditor claims.

🔥 This strategy allows anyone to build generational wealth while staying legally protected and financially secure.

🔥 Chapter 9: The HEFE Family Banking System – Creating Infinite Generational Wealth 🚀

📇 The HEFE Strategy: Building a Family Bank That Lasts for Generations

The HEFE Family Banking System is based on the "ONCE" Strategy (Own Nothing, Control Everything) and follows the multi-generational wealth-building model used by some of the wealthiest families, such as the Rockefellers.

💡 Key Principles of the HEFE System:

✔ Life insurance (IULs) serve as the financial foundation of the trust.

✔ Every child, grandchild, and future generation has an IUL policy owned by the trust.

✔ Trustees ensure that wealth compounds over generations, never being depleted.

✔ Family members can borrow from the trust at specific ages for business or investment opportunities.

✔ Real estate and other assets fund the trust, ensuring continuous financial growth.

🔥 This is how a single generation can build lasting financial security for their bloodline—forever.

HEFE Trust Bylaws: How the System Works for Future Generations

1   Establishing the Trust & Initial Funding

✔ The HEFE Trust is established as an Irrevocable Life Insurance Trust (ILIT) to legally own the IUL policies.

✔ Policies are taken out on every family member—starting with parents, children, and grandchildren.

✔ The trust is funded by income-generating assets (real estate, investments, businesses, etc.).

✔ Some properties are held long-term; others are sold, and proceeds are deposited into a brokerage account to compound over time.

2   Borrowing Rules: Accessing the Trust's Wealth at Key Ages

💰 At Age 13:

✔ Children can borrow from the trust for a business venture if they present a business plan to the trustees.

✔ This teaches financial responsibility, entrepreneurship, and accountability at an early age.

💰 At Age 18:

✔ Trust members receive their first financial education course to prepare them for managing assets.

✔ They can borrow for higher education, trade school, or real estate investments.

💰 At Age 21:

✔ Members can access trust funds for major investments—real estate, starting a business, or wealth-building strategies.

✔ The trust ensures they are financially literate before accessing the full benefits.

🔥 This ensures each generation continues to grow the wealth rather than spend it.

📈 The Power of Compound Interest in Multi-Generational Wealth

One of the most powerful components of the HEFE Family Banking System is compound interest. This ensures that the trust never depletes its funds but instead grows exponentially over time.

💡 Example of Compound Interest Over Generations:

1   ▢ First Generation Funds the Trust

A total of $1,000,000 is deposited into a brokerage account under the trust.

The account earns an average return of 6% per year (a conservative growth estimate).

Over 21 years, the account grows to approximately $3.8 million.

2 ▢ Second Generation (Grandchildren) Receive Half, The Other Half Grows Further

Instead of receiving the full $3.8M, grandchildren only receive 50%—which is $1.9M.

The remaining $1.9M stays in the account, compounding again at 6% for another 21 years.

By the time the next generation (great-grandchildren) reaches 21, the account has grown to $6.7M.

3 ▢ Third Generation (Great-Grandchildren) Repeat the Process

The great-grandchildren only take 50% of the $6.7M—so they receive $3.35M.

The remaining $3.35M stays in the account, compounding again at 6% for another 21 years.

By the time the fourth generation (great-great-grandchildren) reaches 21, the account has now grown to $12.5M.

🔥 In just three generations, an initial $1M investment has turned into over $12.5M—without any new contributions!

✔ This process continues forever.

✔ Each generation receives financial benefits while the principal keeps growing.

✔ Every new generation follows the same structure, ensuring infinite wealth.

📌 Why This Works:

✔ The money is never fully depleted—it always reinvests.

✔ Each generation benefits while ensuring the trust never runs out of funds.

✔ Wealth continues to grow exponentially, even without additional deposits.

🔥 This is the secret to how the Rockefeller Trust has lasted 11+ generations and counting.

🏢 Real Estate & Business Investments: How the Trust Funds Itself

✔ The HEFE Trust acquires real estate and businesses that generate passive income.

✔ Profits from these assets are reinvested into the trust,

ensuring long-term growth.

✔ Each generation is required to contribute to the trust through investments or business earnings.

📌 Example:

The trust purchases 10 rental properties, generating $20,000/month in rental income.

That income funds IUL policies, pays out loans, and increases the trust's total value.

The trust ensures that all real estate is properly managed, so assets continue to appreciate.

🔥 By continuously reinvesting profits, the family never runs out of wealth.

📜 Letter of Trust: Documenting the Family Legacy for Future Generations

Every family member in the trust receives a Letter of Trust—a handwritten document that explains the vision, values, and purpose of the HEFE Family Banking System.

✔ This letter ensures that future generations understand the importance of maintaining the trust.

✔ It provides a personal message from the founder, reminding heirs of their responsibilities.

✔ It is updated every three years to reflect any changes or additions to the system.

📌 Example Letter of Trust Statement:"To my children, grandchildren, and all future heirs of the HEFE Trust—this system was created to ensure that our family never experiences financial hardship. This trust is not just about money; it is about responsibility, legacy, and preserving our name for generations to come. It is your duty to honor these principles and continue the work we have started. Own nothing, control everything, and always reinvest in the future."

🔥 This letter creates an emotional connection to the wealth system, ensuring its longevity.

🚀 Summary: The HEFE Family Banking System – Wealth That Never Dies

✔ Every family member has an IUL policy that funds the trust tax-free.

✔ Borrowing rules ensure financial responsibility, entrepreneurship, and investment knowledge.

✔ Real estate and business assets generate continuous income for the trust.

✔ Offshore banking provides asset protection and tax-efficient growth.

✔ A Letter of Trust documents the family vision, ensuring future generations uphold the system.

✔ The trust grows through compound interest, ensuring wealth increases with every generation.

🔥 This strategy guarantees that wealth compounds over generations, creating an unbreakable financial legacy.

🔥 Chapter 10: Corporate Governance & Robert's Rules of Order – Running a C-Corp the Right Way 🚀

Why Corporate Governance Matters

Starting a **C-Corp** isn't just about getting funding and building wealth—it's also about **running the company correctly** to stay legally compliant and protect the business from liability. Proper corporate governance ensures that:

✔ The company **operates professionally and legally.**

✔ Shareholders and board members **understand their roles and responsibilities.**

✔ The business maintains **corporate veil protection** (so personal assets aren't at risk).

✔ The corporation qualifies for **funding, government contracts, and tax benefits.**

To do this, every successful corporation follows a structured set of rules for meetings, decision-making, and documentation. This system is called Robert's Rules of Order.

📓 What Are Robert's Rules of Order?

🔥 Robert's Rules of Order is the gold standard for how corporations, government entities, and organizations run their meetings.

✔ It ensures that every meeting follows a structured process.

✔ It prevents confusion, disorder, and disputes within the company.

✔ It allows shareholders, board members, and executives to make decisions in an organized and professional way.

✔ Even the U.S. Congress follows Robert's Rules when passing legislation!

📅 How to Run a Proper Corporate Meeting

A C-Corp must hold annual shareholder meetings and board of directors' meetings to stay legally compliant.

📌 Key Meeting Types & Their Purpose

1 ◻ Shareholder Meetings (Annual & Special Meetings)

✔ Held at least once a year to discuss major business decisions.

✔ Shareholders elect the board of directors and vote on key issues.

2 ⬜ Board of Directors Meetings

✔ The board makes high-level strategic decisions about the company.

✔ They appoint executives like the CEO, CFO, and Treasurer.

3 ⬜ Executive Meetings (Management Meetings)

✔ The CEO and management team make operational decisions.

✔ These meetings cover daily business operations, finance, and strategy.

📝 How to Hold a Corporate Meeting Using Robert's Rules

Step 1: Call the Meeting to Order

📌 Example: "The meeting of HEFE 360 GLOBAL INC is now in session."

Step 2: Roll Call & Verify Attendance

📌 The corporate secretary takes attendance and records who is present.

Step 3: Review & Approve the Previous Meeting's Minutes

📌 The board reviews the written record of the last meeting and votes to approve it.

Step 4: Discuss Key Business Issues

📌 Each topic follows a structured process:

✔ A motion is made (example: "I motion to approve the budget for Q2.")

✔ The motion is seconded (another member supports it: "I second the motion.")

✔ Discussion occurs (board members debate the issue).

✔ A vote is held (majority wins, and the secretary records the decision).

Step 5: Closing the Meeting

📌 Once all business is addressed, the chairperson motions to adjourn, and the meeting is closed.

📌 Example: "I motion to adjourn the meeting. Is there a second? The meeting is now closed."

🔥 This structured process ensures that every corporate decision is properly documented and legally binding.

📜 How to Write & Maintain Corporate Meeting Minutes

📌 Meeting minutes are the official record of everything discussed and decided during corporate meetings.

📌 What Should Be Included in Corporate Minutes?

✔ Date & Time of Meeting

✔ Names of Attendees

✔ Motions Made & Who Proposed Them

✔ Voting Results & Final Decisions

✔ Action Items & Next Steps

📝 Example of Proper Corporate Meeting Minutes

📅 Date: March 20, 2025

📌 Location: HEFE 360 GLOBAL INC Headquarters

📝 Meeting Summary

1   🔲 Meeting Called to Order at 10:00 AM

✔ Chairperson: Aaron Hicks (CEO)

2   ☐ Roll Call

✔ Present: Aaron Hicks (Manager), John Doe (Treasurer), Board Members

3   ☐ Approval of Previous Meeting Minutes

✔ Motion by Aaron Hicks to approve minutes from February 2025.

✔ Seconded by John Doe

✔ Motion approved unanimously.

4   ☐ Discussion Topics:

✔ Corporate Budget Approval – Motion to approve a $250,000 budget for Q2. Approved 4-1.

✔ New Business Credit Line – Motion to apply for a $500,000 business line of credit. Approved 3-2.

5   ☐ Meeting Adjourned at 11:30 AM

📌 Secretary Signature: _____

📌 Date Approved: _____

🔥 Proper minutes ensure the corporation stays legally compliant and maintains corporate veil protection.

🏛 Corporate Resolutions & Resolution Letters: Authorizing Major Business Actions

📌 What is a Corporate Resolution?

✔ A corporate resolution is a formal decision made by the board of directors or shareholders.

✔ It is legally binding and must be recorded in the company's minutes.

📌 What is a Resolution Letter?

✔ A resolution letter is a formal request that the corporation uses to ask permission from its board or shareholders to perform an action, such as applying for a loan, opening a new bank account, or making a major purchase.

✔ This document shows banks, lenders, and business partners that the corporation has approved a particular action.

Example Resolution Letter for Business Loan

Date: March 20, 2025

Resolution Number: 2025-002

Resolution to Apply for Business Credit

To Whom It May Concern,

I, Aaron Hicks, CEO of HEFE 360 GLOBAL INC, do hereby certify that at a meeting of the Board of Directors duly held on March 20, 2025, the following resolution was adopted:

"RESOLVED THAT:

✔ The corporation is authorized to apply for a business line of credit in the amount of $500,000.

✔ The Treasurer, John Doe is authorized to sign and submit all necessary documents on behalf of the corporation.

✔ This resolution shall remain in effect until further notice."

CERTIFIED BY:

Signed: _____ (CEO)

Date Approved: _____

🔥 Resolution letters are crucial for securing funding, opening corporate accounts, and making major financial moves.

📓 Every Family Should Own a Copy of Robert's Rules of Order

📌 Robert's Rules of Order is the ultimate guide to running a professional corporation.

✔ It covers everything from conducting meetings to handling voting disputes.

✔ Even government organizations use it to maintain order and efficiency.

✔ Every corporate officer and board member should have a copy.

📌 Where to Get Robert's Rules of Order:

✔ Available on Amazon, Barnes & Noble, and bookstores.

✔ Free PDF versions can be found online.

🔥 This book is essential for running a successful corporation!

🚀 Summary: Mastering Corporate Governance & Running a Business the Right Way

✔ Follow Robert's Rules of Order to run structured meetings.

✔ Maintain proper meeting minutes to stay compliant.

✔ Use resolution letters to request and approve major business actions.

✔ Own a copy of Robert's Rules of Order to ensure professional corporate governance.

🔥 With these principles in place, a corporation operates like a true wealth-building machine.

📖 Chapter 11: Case Studies & Real-World Examples of Generational Wealth 🚀

🏛 How the Wealthy Preserve & Grow Their Money for Generations

While many people focus on making money, the truly wealthy focus on keeping and growing wealth over generations. The biggest difference between the wealthy and the average person is the way they use trusts, corporate finance, and financial leverage.

In this chapter, we will explore real-life case studies of how some of the most successful families and corporations have structured their wealth. These examples will reinforce the HEFE strategy and show how powerful these financial tools can be.

🏛 Case Study #1: The Rockefeller Trust – 11+ Generations of Wealth

The Rockefeller family is one of the best examples of how a trust can maintain and expand wealth for over a century.

◆ How John D. Rockefeller Built His Fortune

✔ Founder of Standard Oil, which became one of the most powerful corporations in history.

✔ Used business credit and financial leverage to expand his empire.

✔ Converted his wealth into a family trust to ensure generational wealth.

◆ The Power of the Rockefeller Trust

✔ The trust was structured so that family members never "own" their money outright.

✔ Instead, wealth is held in trust and controlled by trustees.

✔ Family members receive distributions based on performance and trust guidelines.

📌 What This Means:

Rockefeller's wealth didn't get spent down by heirs.

The trust ensured each generation benefited while continuing to grow the fortune.

The family still controls billions of dollars today, over 100 years later.

🔥 Key Lesson: Using a properly structured trust ensures your wealth will outlive you and continue growing indefinitely.

🏛 Case Study #2: The Rothschild Banking Dynasty – Controlling Wealth Without Owning It

The Rothschild family built a financial empire through international banking, corporate finance, and trust structures.

◆ How the Rothschilds Built Their Empire

✔ Established banking institutions across multiple countries.

✔ Specialized in private banking, trust funds, and lending to governments.

✔ Created multi-generational wealth through interlinked trusts and corporate holdings.

◆ The Rothschild Strategy: Own Nothing, Control Everything

✔ Each generation controls assets through trusts and holding companies.

✔ They never directly own wealth, so it can't be taxed, sued, or lost.

✔ They invest in gold, real estate, and private businesses to avoid economic downturns.

📌 What This Means:

The Rothschilds are one of the longest-lasting financial dynasties in history.

They do not appear on "richest person" lists because they do not hold wealth personally.

Their assets are structured in private trusts and offshore accounts for ultimate protection.

🔥 Key Lesson: The best way to protect generational wealth is to own nothing but control everything.

🏛 Case Study #3: How a Modern Entrepreneur Used the HEFE Strategy to Build Generational Wealth

This example highlights how someone today can use the HEFE strategy to build lasting wealth.

◆ Background:

✔ John, an entrepreneur, started with a single real estate investment.

✔ He formed a C-Corp and two trusts following the HEFE model.

✔ He used business credit to fund his real estate purchases.

◆ Strategy Used:

✔ John transferred his properties into Trust 1 (Cayman Islands).

✔ He used the rental income to create promissory notes.

✔ He issued corporate bonds backed by the promissory notes.

✔ He used the bond proceeds to acquire more properties, repeating the cycle.

◆ Results:

✔ After 10 years, John's real estate portfolio was worth $20M.

✔ His trust structure protected his wealth from lawsuits and taxes.

✔ His children and grandchildren will inherit wealth that continues to grow indefinitely.

🔥 Key Lesson: This strategy works for anyone willing to apply financial intelligence, leverage business credit, and use trust structures for long-term security.

🏛 Case Study #4: How Disney Used Corporate Bonds to Finance an Empire

Most people don't realize that Walt Disney built Disneyland using corporate bonds. Instead of using his own money, Disney leveraged debt, financial instruments, and corporate structuring to fund his vision.

◆ How Disney Funded Disneyland Without Using His Own Money

✔ Walt Disney needed millions of dollars to build Disneyland in the 1950s.

✔ Instead of using personal wealth, he issued corporate bonds backed by future park revenue.

✔ Investors purchased the bonds, giving Disney the capital to build the theme park before it even opened.

✔ As Disneyland became profitable, Disney repaid the bonds and continued expanding his empire.

📌 What This Means:

✔ You don't need millions in cash to acquire assets.

✔ Using corporate bonds backed by real revenue streams is one of the best ways to scale a business.

✔ Even major corporations follow the HEFE strategy—using

corporate finance to expand.

🔥 Key Lesson: Instead of using personal savings, use business credit and corporate bonds to build wealth.

📜 Case Study #5: The Infinite Banking Strategy Used by the Wealthy

Many high-net-worth individuals and families use Indexed Universal Life (IUL) policies to create tax-free wealth while maintaining liquidity.

🔶 How the Wealthy Use Life Insurance to Build Generational Wealth

✔ They fund IUL policies with millions in premiums.

✔ The policies grow tax-free and provide a guaranteed tax-free death benefit.

✔ They borrow against the cash value to make investments—without paying taxes or interest to banks.

✔ This ensures their wealth grows exponentially without ever being depleted.

📌 Example:

A high-net-worth individual deposits $1M into an IUL.

The policy grows at 6-8% annually, tax-free.

They borrow $500K from the policy to buy real estate—without paying taxes on the loan.

When they pass away, the IUL pays out $3-5M to their heirs, tax-free.

🔥 Key Lesson: The Infinite Banking strategy ensures that wealth is never lost to taxes, lawsuits, or reckless spending.

🏦 The HEFE Family Banking System: How You Can Replicate These Strategies

Now that we've seen how major families, corporations, and individuals have successfully used financial strategies to preserve and multiply their wealth, let's recap how the HEFE system applies these principles:

✔ Trusts hold your wealth, ensuring legal and financial protection.

✔ Corporate bonds & business credit allow you to expand without using personal funds.

✔ IULs serve as a tax-free, wealth-building tool for future generations.

✔ The HEFE Family Banking System ensures that every generation benefits from compounding wealth.

🔥 The lesson is clear: Generational wealth isn't just for the elite—it's a system anyone can build if they understand and apply the right financial principles.

🚀 Final Thoughts & Next Steps: Implementing the HEFE Strategy

📌 What to Do Next:

✔ Set up your C-Corp & Trust Structure for wealth protection.

✔ Establish business credit and begin leveraging corporate funding.

✔ Use IULs to create a private banking system for your family.

✔ Invest in real estate, business acquisitions, and financial instruments to grow your wealth.

✔ Educate your family and heirs so they understand how to manage and expand the family fortune.

🔥 This book is not just about financial theory—it's about

action. The next step is implementing the HEFE strategy in your own life to create true financial freedom and generational wealth.

🔥 Conclusion: You Now Have the Blueprint for Financial Independence & Legacy Wealth

With the knowledge in this book, you now understand the exact financial systems used by the world's wealthiest families and corporations.

💡 The key is to take action.

💰 You don't need millions to start—just the right strategy.

🏛 The sooner you apply these principles, the sooner you create generational wealth.

🚀 This is your opportunity to build a financial empire. It's time to get started.

About the Author

HEFE 360 GLOBAL INC is a financial education and consulting company committed to empowering the underbanked and undercredited.

Our mission is to break the traditional barriers of wealth by teaching real-world financial strategies, corporate structuring, trust management, and asset protection.

Through our HEFE Wealth Strategy, we equip individuals, families, and entrepreneurs with the knowledge and tools necessary to create, grow, and protect generational wealth.

At HEFE 360 GLOBAL INC, we believe that financial freedom is not a luxury — it's a right.

To learn more or connect with us:

Website: www.hefe360global.com

Email: info@hefe360global.com

"Own Nothing, Control Everything — Build Wealth Beyond Limits."

Coming Soon from HEFE 360 GLOBAL INC

The Private Bond Blueprint

Structuring Wealth Without Wall Street

Learn how to create your own funding system using private placements, promissory notes, and investment-grade corporate bonds — without relying on banks or traditional lenders.

The HEFE 360 Land Contract Playbook

Turning Real Estate into Multi-Million Dollar Funding

Master the strategy of using land contracts, trust structures, and asset-backed notes to unlock massive funding from your real estate deals.

www.ingramcontent.com/pod-product-compliance
Lightning Source LLC
Chambersburg PA
CBHW030531210326
41597CB00014B/1107